BRINGING THE SEAS INSIDE

...iley

...l Baytoff

Scientific American Books is an imprint of W. H. Freeman and Company, 41 Madison Avenue, New York, New York 10010

Library of Congress Cataloging-in-Publication Data
Riley, Linda Capus
Aquarium : bringing the seas inside / by Linda Capus Riley.
p. cm.
Includes glossary and index.
Summary: Describes how different underwater creatures are captured, how public aquariums are designed and built to house them, and the daily care necessary to keep them healthy.
ISBN 0-7167-6509-8 : $17.95
1. Marine aquariums, Public—Juvenile literature.
2. Aquariums, Public—Juvenile literature.
[1. Aquariums, Public.] I. Title.
QL78.5.R54 1993   93-16341
639.3'42—dc20   CIP
                                                  AC

Printed in the United States of America.

10 9 8 7 6 5 4 3 2 1

Photo Credits

Photographs copyright © 1993 by Michael Baytoff, with the following exceptions: Miriam Austerman/Animals, Animals, p. 78; Bob Cranston/Norbert Wu, p.52; Steven J. Krasemann/NHPA, contents (top left and top right); Zig Leszczynski/Animals, Animals, pp.49, 50-51, 76; Linda Capus Riley, pp. 34, 36, 38, 39, 42, 43

CONTENTS

For my mother and father, Vivian and Richmond Riley,
who introduced me to "my ocean."

Acknowledgments

My heartfelt thanks go to the late Bill Donaldson, president of the Philadelphia Zoo, who dreamed of the New Jersey State Aquarium at Camden; and to Dr. Judith Wellington, who brought the dream to life. Thanks also to the hardworking aquarium staff members who let me follow them around; and to Brian DuVall, Frank Steslow, Fran Ansbro, and Caroline Rieders for their patience in reading and rereading the manuscript.

Very special thanks to Sandy DiGiulio, who helped me keep my head above water in countless ways. Thanks also to Maureen George, Rodica Liggett, Denise Hay, Marilyn Frank, and Steve Capus for their support. And hugs and kisses to my daughter Lindsay-Anne, who loves to find the flounders.

INTRODUCTION

When you visit a public aquarium, you become an underwater explorer, discovering creatures that are bizarre, beautiful, and totally different from anything that lives on land. You come face-to-face with giant sharks, delight in the antics of harbor seals, and learn how fish survive in a fish-eat-fish world.

"An aquarium shows people a foreign land that is right there," says Dr. Judith Wellington, chief executive officer of the Thomas H. Kean New Jersey State Aquarium at Camden. "People don't spend a lot of time underwater. It's familiar but foreign."

This book goes one step further, offering an insider's view of how an aquarium brings the seas inside.

Witness the careful capture of the fish; the design and building of their homes away from home; and the daily challenge of keeping the animals healthy and well fed.

See why a shark hunt is an exercise in tenderness, not terror. Meet the seal trainers, the fish doctor, and the divers who swim with the sharks. Discover the wonders and fragility of the underwater world.

1 WONDERS DOWN UNDER

Sharks cruise lazily through a vast expanse of water, sending schools of small spade fish and big striped bass scurrying away. Flounders lie quietly concealed on the ocean floor, while pairs of clearnose skates lift their wings ever so slightly out of the water as they glide along.

Flounders show their white underbellies in a tank that hangs above visitors' heads. Sharks snack on mackerel offered at the end of poles, right before visitors' eyes. And cownose rays slide warily up out of the water for toddlers to touch.

It all began with a guest list of sorts.

Long before the concrete was poured, the windows caulked into place, and the salt-water mixed, a team of habitat designers and marine biologists sat down to make a list of fish.

It was every bit as complicated as deciding whom to invite to a wedding and where to seat the guests:

Blue sharks don't travel well, so there's no sense inviting them; crabs and eels may eat one another, so they can't be together; the octopus is shy and needs a tank of its own; the turtles should be across from the jellyfish where they can look at but not snack on them.

Beyond these practical concerns, the designers wanted the outdoor spaces and first floor to be a tour of many waterways, from mountain streams to the river and down to the sea. They also wanted visitors to see how aquatic animals experience their world.

Gathering all of the "guests" for the new aquarium took close to a full year. The aquarists, or marine animal keepers, had to collect about two thousand different animals

Lumpfish lie so still in their rocky tide pools that the aquarists can just bend down and pick them up.

This is the scene just off the East Coast of the United States. Beneath the surface of these cool gray-green waters lie mysteries usually reserved for the eyes of scuba divers, marine biologists, and seasoned fishermen.

But now, after seven years of planning and construction that cost some $52 million, a new aquarium reveals these mysteries for all to see.

of about 150 species from streams, rivers, tidal pools, and coastal waters.

Some of them wore wet suits and scuba gear, braving fast-moving tides off the coast of Maine to bring back fat northern red anemones and twelve-armed orange sun stars.

Some dipped into the tea-brown cedar waters of New Jersey's Pine Barrens to net banded sunfish, pirate perch, and swamp darters.

Some waded through squishy salt-marsh creeks, braving mosquitoes and crabs to capture slender pipefish and seahorses.

Some netted wayward tropical fish, swept north on the warm Gulf Stream, from the coastal waters off Long Island, New York.

And everyone took a turn at bringing back the sharks.

The aquarium displays a dazzling diversity of aquatic life and habitats, from spotted turtles in the Pine Barrens display to sleek brown sharks and silvery lookdowns in the Open Ocean tank.

BRINGING THEM BACK ALIVE

2

If the idea of fishing for sharks conjures up images of saber-toothed man-eaters lunging for your legs, think again.

"Lots of people on boats go crazy when they catch a shark because it's a shark," says Brian DuVall, an aquarist and director of husbandry for the new aquarium. "But when you work with sharks all the time, you develop a different attitude."

For the last ten years, Brian has swum with sharks, fed them by hand, and studied their habits.

"They're really not dangerous animals—they're not aggressive. When you pull a shark out of the water and put it in the boat, it's not looking for something to bite. It's trying to get away. You can't get hysterical about it."

When he hooks a shark, Brian's challenge has just begun. Unlike most fishermen, Brian must bring the shark back alive and well. And sharks, which have the meanest reputation in the sea, are surprisingly fragile creatures.

A shark's skeleton is not made of hard bone—it is made of cartilage, the same flexible stuff our noses and ears are made from. It does not protect the shark's internal organs quite as well as bone would, even in the water. Under normal conditions, this is not a problem. But when a shark is thrashing around, trying to free itself from a hook, it can suffer serious internal injuries.

Out of the water, the shark's cartilage skeleton is too flexible to be much protection at all—the animal's own body weight can crush its internal organs.

So fishing for an aquarium is very different from fishing for sport or food.

The person who put the hunk of bait fish on the hook passes it to the one feeding the baited line into the water.

Tuckerton, New Jersey
9 A.M. Friday, August 16
Bright-orange ball buoys bob on the dark-gray water of Great Bay, marking the location of a fishing line set last night.

A hose draws water from the bay into a fiberglass transport box about the size of a coffin—seven feet long by two feet high and wide.

Aquarists Fran Ansbro and Jim Brooks scoop buckets of water into the transport

A blue bucket sits on the deck filled with mackerel, tail end up, ready to be chopped up as bait. John Camper (left) and Jim Brooks pull 40 hooks from the clothes basket one by one, baiting them and clipping them to the long line. An orange buoy at each end of the long line marks its position, so the boat can leave this spot to fish elsewhere, then return to see if any sharks have taken the bait.

box, getting ready for the moment when there's a shark on the line.

This is the second day of fishing for the toothy brown sharks that will rule the aquarium's 760,000-gallon Open Ocean tank. These sleek torpedoes grow to be some eight feet long, lurking near the bottom of shallow bays and estuaries and feeding on shellfish, crabs, and fish. Their brown backs and preference for shallow waters give *Carcharhinus plumbeus* their common names: brown shark and sandbar shark.

Brian DuVall steers the Spartina *slowly alongside the long line as John Camper pulls up the hooks one by one to see if they have hooked any sharks. The bait is gone from every hook—probably stolen by crabs.*

Found from Massachusetts to Brazil at varying times of the year, hundreds of brown sharks come into the bays off New Jersey in June each year to give birth to their five-pound pups. After Labor Day, they head south for the winter.

Now the pressure is on. The aquarium's opening day is just six months away. Brian says they hope to get at least eight brown sharks for the Open Ocean tank. And the sharks have to be collected before they head south.

Normally, Brian says, shark fishing is best when the tides are changing and the moving water carries the taste and smell of the bait, tempting the sharks to come and feed.

But the heavy rain two nights ago lowered the salt content in the water, which could cause the sharks to stay out of the bay. Also, the early, hot summer could result in a shortened season, with the sharks heading south earlier than usual.

All the crew can do now is bait the lines and wait.

The long line used to catch sharks is like a nylon clothesline about one thousand feet long, with forty hooks twenty-five feet apart dangling from it. An anchor at each end holds the line in place, and buoys attached to the anchors float on the surface, marking where the line is.

Brian steers the boat as the line is pulled up and checked. The bait is gone from every hook.

"Crabs," Fran says with a frown. Crabs are common bait thieves, and can ruin a fishing trip by grabbing the bait before the fish even get a whiff of it.

Brian talks over the marine radio to the charter boat captain, Dennis Genaro, who is showing the aquarists around his territory for two days. Dennis is bringing the bait in his thirty-foot fishing vessel, *Geri.* He's hauling about two hundred whole mackerel and four big two-foot-tall metal chum buckets—cans filled with chopped-up fish.

The transport box occupies center stage on the twenty-three-foot aquarium boat *Spartina,* leaving a narrow walkway around it. The *Spartina* has a small cabin to shelter the crew, and low sides to ease the problems of hauling in a seven-foot, 150-pound shark.

The *Spartina* pulls up to the *Geri* for bait.

Although most of the aquarists have considerable fishing experience, they rely on Dennis's expertise and knowledge of these waters. For the past twelve years, he has specialized in catching sharks and rays in Great Bay and nearby Little Egg Harbor.

After a brief conference and a transfer of bait, the *Spartina* returns to the long line, and the crew bait the hooks.

Brian takes the lid off the chum bucket,

which is filled with chopped-up menhaden. He jabs holes in the bucket with a big screwdriver. The chum bucket is attached to one end of the long line. For a few hours after it is set, fish oil seeps out and is spread by the breeze across the water's surface. At the same time, chunks of fish float out through holes in the bucket and are carried by the current in another direction. The result is a tasty "slick" that attracts sharks the way the smell of baking draws people into the kitchen.

After setting the long lines, the crew does some hook-and-line fishing without much success.

Along the shore; two white egrets stand calmly in the tall marsh grasses, their long necks stretching as they look curiously over the grass.

2:30 P.M.

Suddenly the radio crackles. "*Spartina; Geri* to *Spartina*; we've got a shark—do you want to come over?"

"Roger that," Brian answers.

The crew springs into action, moving everything possible into the cabin, clearing the sides of the boat.

The boat crashes through the waves. Brian is speeding, searching for sight of the other boat.

Aquarist John Camper gets ready for the shark. Because there is no filter system in the transport box to keep the water clean, he adds three capfuls of Amquel, a mixture that reacts with the ammonia from the shark's wastes, binding it so it can't hurt the animal.

At last the *Spartina* pulls up to the *Geri* and ties up. Dennis is leaning over the bow, holding his rod over the water.

Brian loops a line around the shark's tail to help the crew control its movements. "That's where the shark's power is," he explains. "If you rely on the hook in its mouth, when you pull the hook, you will damage the shark. So you get a tail line on it and pull it alongside the boat."

Instead of lifting the shark or hauling it in on the line as a sport fisherman might do, the aquarists use a canvas stretcher or a net. This evens out the pressure on the shark's body, protecting its heart and other organs from the weight of its own body as it is lifted into the transport box.

This shark is fairly small—only three feet long—so Jim grabs the net, and he and Dennis lift the animal into it. John takes a pair of

Dennis Genaro strains against the pull of a giant ray that led the crew on a five-hour chase. It ran around the boat, under it, away from it, and straight to the bottom, nearly pulling Dennis down with it. Finally, it snapped the line and got away, just as the boat was about to run out of gas.

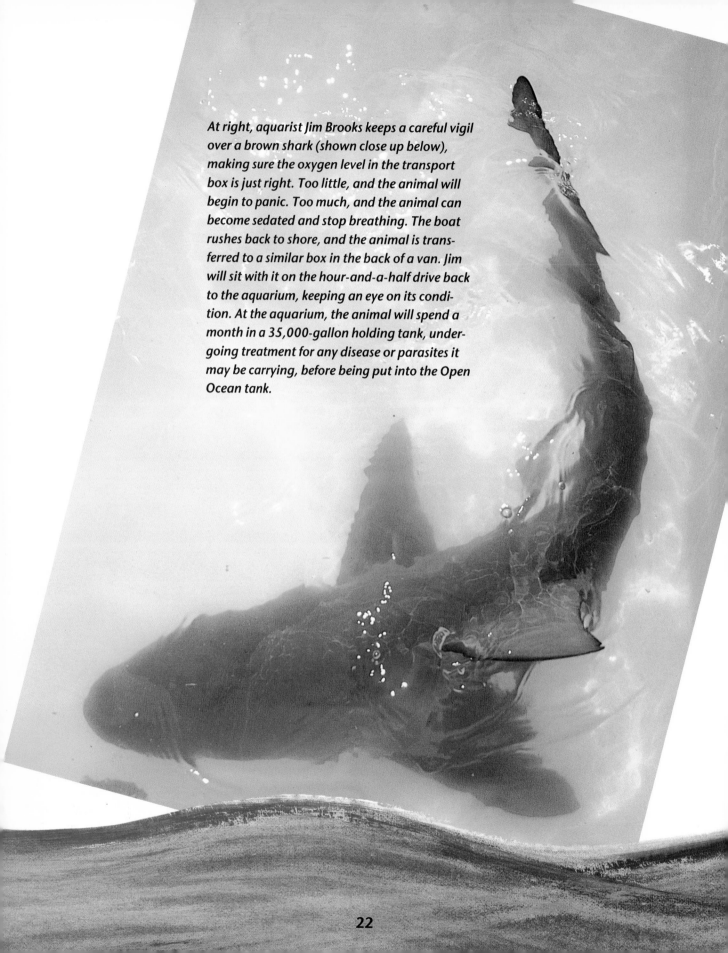

At right, aquarist Jim Brooks keeps a careful vigil over a brown shark (shown close up below), making sure the oxygen level in the transport box is just right. Too little, and the animal will begin to panic. Too much, and the animal can become sedated and stop breathing. The boat rushes back to shore, and the animal is transferred to a similar box in the back of a van. Jim will sit with it on the hour-and-a-half drive back to the aquarium, keeping an eye on its condition. At the aquarium, the animal will spend a month in a 35,000-gallon holding tank, undergoing treatment for any disease or parasites it may be carrying, before being put into the Open Ocean tank.

pliers and cuts the barb from the shark's mouth, then pulls the hook out.

Getting the shark settled down in the box is the next challenge. Many species of sharks are difficult to transport, because if they stop swimming, they can suffocate.

These sharks look menacing because their toothy jaws stay open as they swim. But they're not just looking for lunch—they're breathing, letting water flow into their mouths and over their gills, which take oxygen from the water into their systems. Preventing a shark from swimming by putting it in a box can lower the amount of oxygen it's getting, which can make it panic. So the box has to be set up just right, to provide lots of oxygen. A small pump is installed in the transport box, and the output is directed over the shark.

But the aquarists have to be careful. Pure oxygen injected into the water stream calms the shark, but too much oxygen can act as a sedative and make the shark stop breathing. They keep a close watch to make sure the levels are just right.

"He's doing pretty well," John says. He measures the oxygen and the salt content of the water, then touches the shark's eyes to see if it reacts.

Brian asks if it's breathing.

"Yes," says John. "We've got a shark—a small one, but it's a shark!"

3
FISH ARE JUMPIN'

The moon is still high in the sky as a pink buoy of a sun bobs up on the horizon. Charter boat captain Bill Garrison's thirty-foot boat, the *Sea Mist*, is heading out for sharks and whatever else can be found.

Summer is waning, and the pressure is increasing. Many fish, including the sharks, have started to head south for the winter.

Cape May, New Jersey
7 A.M. Saturday, August 31

The boat reaches the spot at the mouth of Delaware Bay where the long line will be set.

Fifteen-year-old Jamie Manning, Bill's first mate, drops first the buoy, then the anchor, overboard. Seventeen-year-old Jason Brown baits the hooks, and aquarist Marc Kind tosses them overboard, one by one.

The crew motors a bit, then cuts the engines and begins fishing.

Jamie baits and casts a double hook. He has a bite immediately—two jacks. He repeats the motion three times, four. Each time he catches two more fish.

"We're going to get you a school of jacks," Bill shouts excitedly.

Marc looks them up in a guidebook—they're *Seriola dumerili*, commonly known as greater amberjacks. Each has a stripe from the tip of the nose through its eye to the dorsal, or back, fin.

These are no more than a foot long now, but they can grow to be five feet long and can weigh over 175 pounds.

"They hang around the lobster pots," Bill says. "We just call them buoy jacks."

Skip Uricchio stirs up the water in the transport box to increase its oxygen content.

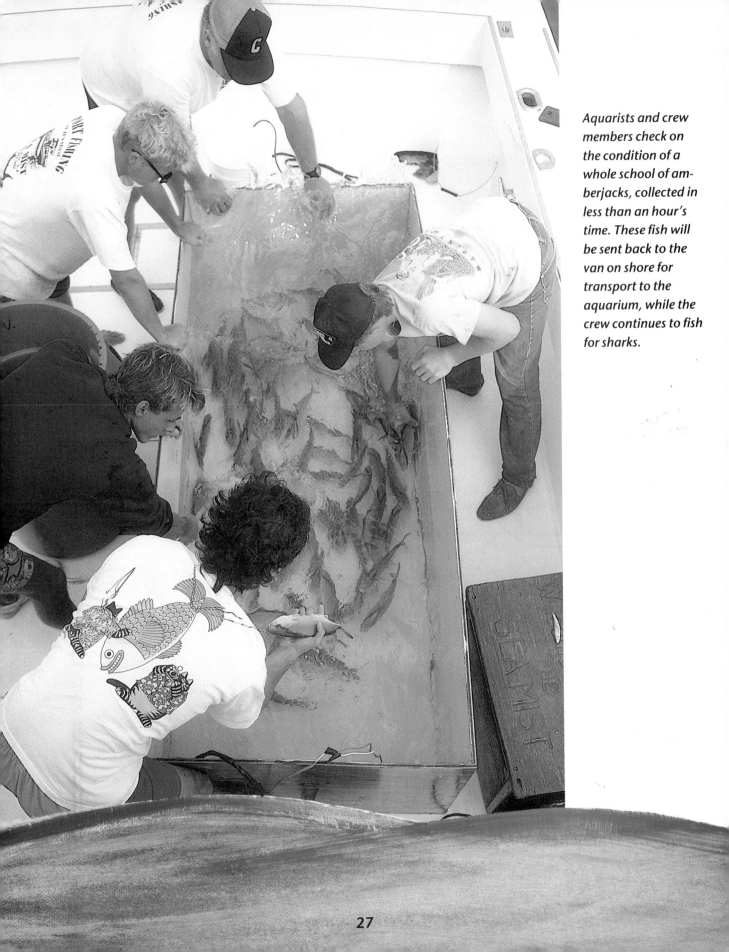

Aquarists and crew members check on the condition of a whole school of amberjacks, collected in less than an hour's time. These fish will be sent back to the van on shore for transport to the aquarium, while the crew continues to fish for sharks.

The sound of thunder rolls in from the shore. The boat rolls and pitches, and the crew members have put on yellow slicker overalls. They are pulling in the long line.

Up comes a small brown cownose ray about two feet across. Marc carefully takes the hook from its mouth and drops it into the transport box. He pulls in a small clearnose skate, its back mottled like tortoiseshell. The two lie placidly at opposite corners on the bottom of the box.

Jamie pulls toward the buoy at the other end of the line. As he reaches the end, he pulls in another skate.

A skate bites Marc's finger as he pulls it in and takes it off the hook.

The *Delta Lady* riverboat cruises by. The captain tells the passengers to check out the fish in the tank.

"Captain Bill Garrison and the aquarium," he announces. The *Sea Mist* crew waves to the riverboat passengers, who wave back and cheer.

The clearnose skate has dental plates to mash its food.

"About one third of the species found in Shinnecock Bay at this time of year are summer tropical visitors," Captain Bruce Ringerz tells a group of ten high school juniors as they pull away from the dock on a trimaran pontoon boat.

The tropical fish found here don't migrate, he explains. They are accidental tourists.

"Butterflyfish, angelfish, lookdowns—they start their journey as

They may look like eyes, but those holes on either side of the skate's head are nostrils. Its real eyes are on top of its head.

egg masses, get caught up in the Gulf Stream, and find themselves far from home. They won't survive the winter here," he says.

Fran waits on the beach with aquarist Randy Mickley as the boat pulls in close to shore. Five of the students splash off the boat, holding one end of a net that is a hundred feet long and about eight feet high and is held sideways like a volleyball net. Bruce pulls the boat down the beach and drops off the rest of the students with the other end of the net.

Weights hold the bottom of the net down and floats keep the top up as they drag it slowly in to shore.

When the students open the net, at first it looks like just a mass of eelgrass—then the fish begin to flop around.

"Treat the fish as delicately as possible," Bruce cautions. "If you remove the slime coat or the scales, it's as injurious to the fish as if somebody used a knife to take the first couple layers of your skin off."

There are little snappers, a blackfish, and a spotted coronetfish.

Fran combs through the seaweed with her fingers and picks up what looks like a leaf—it's an inch-long bright-green fish. "This may be a parrotfish," she says, dipping it into a bucket.

Another drag nets a trumpetfish, a bluefish, a silvery lookdown, a pale-yellow

(top) Aquarists Fran Ansbro and Randy Mickley drag their net onto a Long Island beach.

(bottom) The aquarists always use a net with small holes. One with larger holes would tear the fins and gills of large fish and would let tiny fish like these silversides through.

banded butterflyfish the size of a silver dollar, and a half-inch-long permit.

"Those get huge—they're popular sport fish," Randy says, picking up the permit.

Buckets are carried back to the truck; bags are filled with water. Randy shoots oxygen through a tube into a bag of seahorses. The water burbles and bubbles, and the bag inflates like a balloon. He fastens it with a rubber band.

Fran gently picks up a handful of pipefish that wriggle like living noodles and dips them into a bag.

She mixes Amquel and pink Polyaqua, a vitamin-rich mixture that restores the slime coat. These will keep the fish healthy for the four-hour ride home.

Eastport, Maine
6 A.M. Wednesday, October 23

In search of five-armed blood stars, prickly green sea urchins, and giant sun stars, Fran and Marc have driven north to Maine.

Checking the tide tables carefully, they get up early to go tidepooling. Wading in the changeable areas along the rocky shoreline where land meets sea, they flip rocks over to find colorful anemones, animals whose delicate, waving tentacles make them look like exotic flowers. Here, lumpfish cling to rocks in the shallow water, and finicky Acadian hermit crabs scuttle about on the bottom.

"These hermit crabs usually have extra shells," Fran says, picking one up. "They like to switch, and they're always looking for a more comfortable shell. But they don't just pop in—first they spend a couple of hours cleaning it out."

Later in the day they prepare for a dive into deeper waters off the rocky coast.

"I've collected here before," Fran says. "It's a tricky spot to dive, but I know we can get what we want."

Timing is critical because the tide changes here are sudden and dramatic, with the water level changing by about thirty feet between high and low tides.

"We have to go in right at slack tide—the hour when the tide is lowest and hasn't started to come in yet," says Fran. "And we have to get out before the tide comes in, because when it does, it comes screaming by the buoy. You'd be hanging on like a flag."

Marc and Fran check the tide tables and get to the dive site at least an hour before slack low tide.

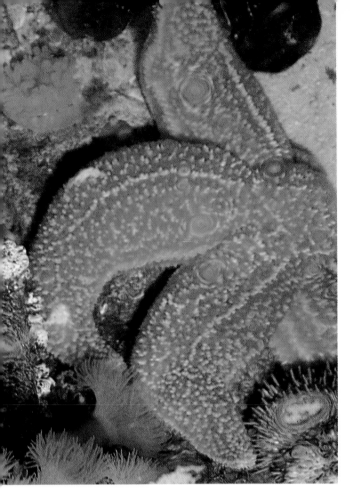

Carrying their dive gear, they climb down over the slippery, algae-covered rocks around thirty feet from the road. At the waterline, they pull on wetsuits, hoods, and cold-water mitts that leave just a finger and thumb free. They strap on their tanks, pull on their masks, and finally step into their fins.

Holding mesh collecting bags, they splash awkwardly into the water, then go under, always keeping an eye on each other.

On the first dive they follow a wall of rock down to a depth of about forty feet, swimming and looking.

Coming across a northern red anemone, Fran wedges her finger under it and peels it gently off the rock. If she finds one attached to a loose rock, she takes the whole rock.

Marc and Fran fill up two bags each, then head back for shore, where they have a cooler filled with water.

"The sun stars were hard to find underwater because of the red color," Fran says. "Red is the first color to disappear. I look for the shape—the silhouette. And then getting them in the bag is something else. It's hard to handle them with these cold-water mitts. The spines stick to them. And it's really hard to open and close the clips on the collecting bags."

"The sculpins look just like rocks," Marc says. "The bottom is covered with them. I just grab them behind their heads—they don't even see me coming."

The aquarium has no holding area here, so Fran and Marc take the animals to a nearby pier, put them in traps, and leave them in the water until they're ready to go home.

They lose about twenty northern sea stars overnight. "They must have gotten out of the trap holes one leg at a time," Fran says. "They're very patient creatures."

4
HOMES AWAY FROM HOME

While the aquarists are busy fishing, workers are hurrying to finish new homes for the fish in time for opening day. Fish collected before the aquarium is ready are held in special tanks at a nearby warehouse while work on the exhibits is completed.

Some workers craft a cave for the octopus, while others plant artificial eelgrass for the seahorses. A sandy beach is prepared for the shorebirds, and a rocky shore readied for the seals.

"We're not just creating tanks with pretty fish in them. We're creating an experience," says exhibit specialist Joe Wetzel. "A museum or aquarium is like a walk-through play. You change the lighting, raise or lower the ceiling, make some parts bright and friendly, others dark and mysterious, and that's how you build surprise and drama."

The aquarium will unfold like a storybook, as visitors journey from deep ocean waters to a sunken shipwreck, then emerge on a sandy beach. But the architects and designers had more to consider than just the story line. An aquarium is built to serve three different audiences: the visitors, the staff, and the fish.

Traffic studies are done, to see what route visitors would take and how many people the building could hold. Windows are built wide enough for a crowd, and low enough to give a child or a person in a wheelchair a good view. Models are made of the service spaces behind the scenes to make sure that the aquarists will have enough elbow room to dip nets on eight-foot-long handles into the tanks.

A crane hoists the heavy folds of a tent roof over the huge Open Ocean tank. Workers balance on the building's upper rim, preparing to stretch it tight and fasten it securely.

Skylights over the Barrier Beach exhibit provide the natural light that the birds need to thrive. A canvas roof stretches over the Open Ocean tank like a huge circus tent, to let daylight drift in. And crevices carved into the thirteen-foot wall of rock at the Edge of the Abyss exhibit in the Open Ocean tank will make the sculpins feel right at home.

A Giant Fish Tank

The huge two-story Open Ocean tank will be the centerpiece of the aquarium's exhibits. Building, stocking, and maintaining it present challenges on a grand scale.

But this is more than just a big fish tank. For one thing, there is its shape. "The first big tanks built were doughnut-shaped raceways. The fish had to swim in the same direction, in a circular route. Round tanks were not conducive to shark health because the sharks were swimming in circles all the time," says architect Steve McDaniel.

"Experts told us that in an enclosure sharks swim in a kind of figure-eight pattern, so we tried to design a tank that would

This is one of the largest fish tanks in the country, measuring 120 feet across at one point—about the distance from home plate to second base on a baseball diamond. It is 77 feet across at its widest point, and its deepest section, called the Abyss, for the deepest part of the ocean, is 24 feet deep. Its 760,000 gallons of water would be enough to fill up a standard-sized 33-gallon bathtub every night for almost 65 years.

accommodate that," Steve explains. "If you draw two squares and place them point to point, then slide them together so they overlap, you'll see the shape of this tank."

The tank's size will create the illusion of the ocean's vastness, where sharks can be seen swimming from a distance, then looming up right in front of a window. And these are no ordinary windows.

Workers watch a 30,000-pound window being lifted into place.

Vast Views of the Ocean Floor

Workers standing at the foot of the Edge of the Abyss exhibit are dwarfed by an opening two stories tall that will hold the biggest window ever made.

The giant acrylic window is 24 feet wide by 18 feet high and is 12 5/8 inches thick. It was made in three pieces that were then joined together so cleanly, you have to look closely to find the seam.

It's a sunny, blustery day when the window on the Abyss is ready to be put in place. Construction workers put down their drills and saws and line up along the top of the big ocean tank with their cameras.

"I've never seen anything this big," says one of thirty glaziers, workers whose trade is setting glass. Normally, the weight of a piece of glass determines how many glaziers are needed to set it. But at thirty thousand pounds, this window is too big for any number of workers to lift, so a crane has been brought in to do the job.

Slowly, ever so slowly, the huge window is lifted off the tractor trailer bed until it's upright in the air, the sunlight glinting off its thick edges. Workers hold their breath as the window is lifted up and over the outside wall of the building. Then the cranes lower it down into the canyon that forms the Edge of the Abyss drop-off in the ocean tank.

As the window nears the opening, glaziers on the tank's floor guide it into place and a cheer goes up.

But the best view in the world won't help if the water won't stay in the tank.

Plugging the Cracks

One chilly morning, construction manager George Mote walks around the outside of the ocean tank, looking for puddles and cracks. Much to his disappointment, he finds some.

"Concrete does two things—it gets hard and it cracks," George says. "It's normal that shrinkage cracks develop in concrete. But if the salt water from the tank gets into those cracks, it can rust the reinforcing steel. The steel then expands and can break the concrete apart. Our steel is coated with epoxy to try to prevent that."

The floor of the ocean tank is made of concrete thirty inches thick; most of the walls are two feet thick. Waterproofing it has been one

Brian DuVall stands above the Open Ocean tank, watching the water level rise. A year from now, visitors will peer through the portholes as seven-foot sharks, stingrays, and striped bass glide by. But right now, workers are worried about finding and fixing any cracks, to keep the water inside.

of the construction crew's biggest challenges.

"Probably more work has gone into this than anything else," George says. "It's not a science—there is no tried-and-true method. And whatever we use has to be tough enough to hold up well underwater, tough enough to stay on the walls—but it can't harm the animals."

Three different waterproofing plans are tried before the tank holds water. The final solution to the problem is to paint on layer after layer of plastic resin.

"It's nice and flexible, so if the tank settles and cracks develop, it will stretch," says assistant project manager Ernie Miller. "And unlike bare concrete, it forms a smooth surface, so the fish won't get scraped if they rub against it."

After six months of experimentation, the tank holds water. Now it is time for the finishing touches that will turn a huge concrete vault into the ocean realm: custom-made rocks and a sunken ship covered with mussels so tasty looking, the fish will try to eat them.

A tautog lurking at the bottom of the shipwreck discovers that those tasty-looking mussels are artificial.

Fooling the Fish

Sea stars will cling to rock cliffs, barnacles and shiny black mussels will vie for living space on timber pilings, and a shipwreck on the bottom will seem to slowly rust away.

But it will all be a carefully crafted illusion.

Of some fifty sea stars that will dot the rocks in exhibits throughout the aquarium, little more than a handful will have been plucked from the ocean. The rest will come to life as sculptures, poured into molds.

Even the rocks they'll cling to won't be real. More than ten thousand concrete blocks form the base for the underwater rockwork in the Open Ocean tank. Preformed concrete panels molded from real rock formations will be fastened on top of the concrete block. After that, the joints will be filled in and the rock face sculpted into convincing curves and painted to create the final illusion.

"Real rock would be cheaper, but a pile of real rocks looks like a pile of rocks. We make rock formations," says Andy Anderson about the habitats his company creates.

These mini-worlds are made from the most unglamorous of materials. Concrete blocks and fiberglass panels are shaped into towering rock formations. Artists sculpt plastic into delicate brain corals and clumps of mussels that will cling to a fiberglass ocean pier.

And the shipwreck? Not only was it not dredged from the sea—it will be in no danger of rusting. There won't be a scrap of metal on it. It's all made of fiberglass, right down to the rivets.

"A real wreck in an aquarium tank would destroy the water quality. Heavy metals in the water can kill the fish," Andy says. "This will go together a lot like a real boat. We'll build the centerline, then the ribs that give the shape of the hull. And then we'll start to age it, by adding thickened resins that give the effect of rust scaling off it. Then we start encrusting marine growth—first sponges and algae, then mussels."

The process takes place in much the same order as it would in nature, only faster. Instead of taking years to deteriorate, it takes a few weeks. Then it is shipped to the aquarium and sunk for good.

After the mountains are made and the shipwreck put in place, there will be two more test fills to make sure the rock installation did not damage the waterproofing. Then it will be time to mix up saltwater soup.

Saltwater Soup

For six days and nights, city water flows from a fire hydrant through a special tractor trailer with filters inside of it that purify the water. Then it is pumped into the aquarium's Open Ocean tank through a two-and-a-half-inch hose.

41

Aquatic biologist Frank Steslow watches as 760,000 gallons of water seep slowly into the Open Ocean tank. Puddles begin to form on the sandy bottom, and water cascades over the shipwreck and the rockwork.

"We can't use real seawater because it would be too expensive to get it here," Frank says. "Aquariums that are near the sea can pump seawater right into their exhibits. We don't have direct access to salt water; we're

Skip Uricchio uses a shovel to stir up chemicals being added to create the 760,000 gallons of salt water for the Open Ocean tank.

The water in the aquarium circulates continuously though several kinds of filters to remove wastes and any other harmful substances. This picture shows the bio towers—huge cylinders on the aquarium's roof that are filled with small plastic balls called bio balls. Bacteria living on the bio balls consume the ammonia from the fish wastes, breaking it down and cleaning the water.

on a river, which is fresh water. So we've taken one of the published formulas for salt water and adjusted it to fit the needs of the fish that will live in the ocean tank."

First ingredient of the formula: lots of salt. A huge cylindrical tank truck pulls up alongside the building. Workers attach a heavy hose, which is snaked up over the roof and into the holding pool at the side of the ocean tank.

The flick of a switch starts a blower that will run for two days, pumping 160,000 pounds of table salt into the water—the first ingredient of "saltwater soup."

Blowing in the 160,000 pounds of salt is the easy part. The 100,000 pounds of other chemicals are added by hand. Aquarists Fran Ansbro, Skip Uricchio, and Jim Brooks hoist bag after hundred-pound bag of chemicals,

slit them open, and dump them in.

Some are mixed into a small tank at the edge of the holding pool and stirred with a shovel; others are dumped directly into the pool that opens onto the ocean tank. The aquarists work steadily for hours, wearing dust masks to protect themselves from the white clouds of chemicals that fill the air as the bags are dumped.

Most of the chemicals dissolve as they drift through the water. But some cake up on the bottom, so Skip pulls on his wet suit and climbs down into the pool with a rake to mix things up a bit.

Once Frank is satisfied that the mix is right, aquarists can begin to move the fish from their temporary homes at the warehouse into the new aquarium, in preparation for opening day.

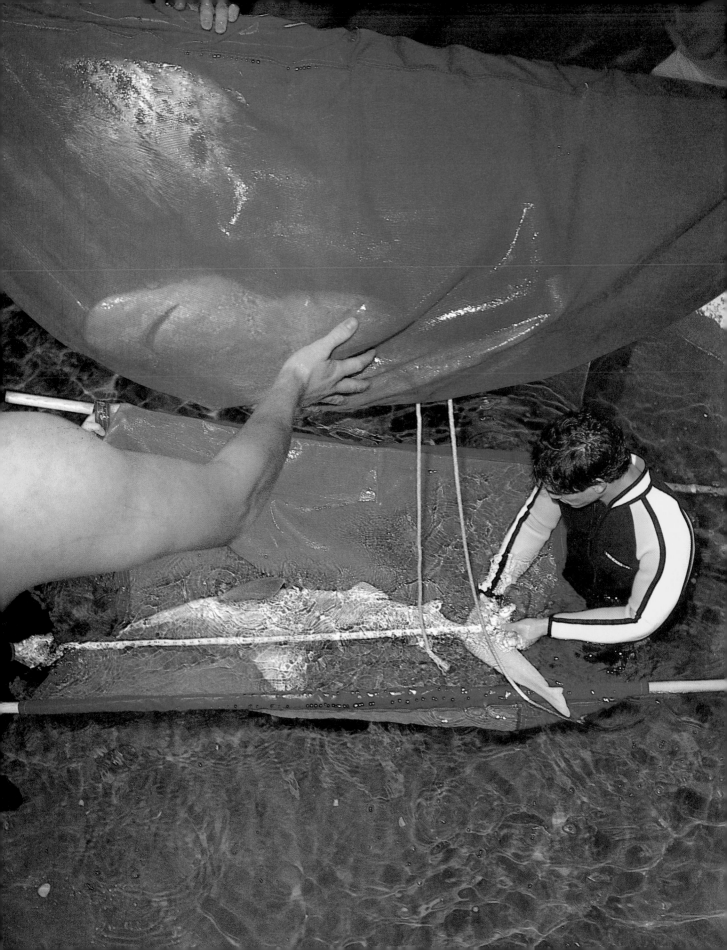

5
IS THERE A DOCTOR IN THE TANK?

Keeping the water clean makes Frank Steslow's other job—doctoring the fish—a lot simpler. But there's no way to wipe out all illnesses. And when the fish get sick, making a "house call" is sometimes the only way the doctor has of catching up with his patients.

When treating the sharks, the first choice is always to get the animal to come to the doctor. With that in mind, the aquarists train the sharks to eat fish attached to the end of a twenty-foot-long pole. The aquarists stand on the catwalk above the ocean tank and put the pole into the water.

Feeding time gives the aquarists a chance to make sure each shark is eating right and to get a close-up look to spot any medical problems. If there are problems, medicine can be added to the food—or the mackerel can be used as a lure if hands-on treatment is required.

"If a shark is sick and we need to get it out, we can lure it into the acclimation tank with food and close the gate," Frank says. The acclimation tank is a small area attached to the big ocean tank but separated from it by a gate, so new animals can get used to their surroundings slowly, or sick ones can be nursed back to health.

Once the shark is in the acclimation tank, the doctor can give it a shot in the saddle of muscles behind its dorsal, or back, fin, using a needle on the end of a pole. The shot puts the animal to sleep. Aquarists can use a stretcher to lift it gently from the water for examination.

But often a sick animal stops feeding or won't cooperate. Then Frank has to take the plunge. "If I really have to, I can dive in with a pole syringe, give the shark anesthetic, and physically pull it out," he says.

Fish Physicals

Figuring out what's wrong is a real challenge when your patients can't tell you what hurts. Body language is often the only clue that a fish is sick.

"I look for strained swimming behavior, abnormal breathing, listlessness, poor appetite," Frank says.

Each morning Frank makes his rounds, first at the warehouse, then at the aquarium, stopping at every window to check on the fish. Of some four hundred fish in the Open Ocean tank, there may be a handful that have problems. Spotting those problems early and treating them promptly keeps the rest of the fish healthy—just as a child who has chicken pox is kept home from school.

A striped sea bass.

"Lately you can see a lot of the sea bass and stripers constantly yawning—stretching their mouths," Frank says, pointing out a school of stripers in the Open Ocean tank. "Sometimes that's a natural stretch, but it could also be a gill parasite. It's something I'll have to keep an eye on.

"Another sign of parasites is scratching and flashing—kind of twitching in mid-water, or rubbing against the rocks or sand. These are signs that the animal is trying to rub off external parasites. If you had a piece of ocean this clear, with this number of fish, you would see them flashing. Parasites are just part of their life," Frank says.

Aquatic biologist Frank Steslow holds a loggerhead turtle gently while giving it eye drops.

Parasites on a fish are like fleas on a dog. The dog can stand a few fleas; but if the animal is sick or old, it can't keep them under control. The animal's weakness gives the fleas a chance to multiply to the point where they can do serious harm.

The confined space of the aquarium presents a problem, because once the parasites have gotten in, they can multiply and take over more quickly than they would in the ocean.

Fish play host to many kinds of parasites. Copepods, which look like small crabs, burrow into the fishes' gills. Other parasites are

If a fish dies, Frank Steslow will do a necropsy, cutting it open and examining its organs and flesh to find the cause of its death.

so tiny, they live inside an animal's cells, and Frank has to do lab tests to make a diagnosis.

"I'll do a skin scraping—scrape some mucus onto a slide and look at it under a microscope. I can see very small parasites that way," he says.

"If I don't see anything in a scraping of mucus, I can sacrifice one fish to do a necropsy—the fish version of an autopsy. I take a snip of the gills—they're where a lot of diseases enter the fish. Internally, I'll look at the organs and body tissues."

Sacrificing one fish can save many. Once he knows what's wrong, Frank can treat the other fish before the disease becomes too widespread.

A red drum sitting on a rock catches his eye. "See how that fish is half dark-red and half light-red, just hanging there listlessly over the rock? It's not doing well. If it's still there when the divers go in later, I'll get them to net it out."

This is the second sick red drum he's noticed. But the divers didn't get a chance to net the last one—a shark bagged it first.

"The red drum had been sitting on a rock, looking really listless. I was waiting for it to die so I could do a necropsy and see what was wrong," Frank says. "All of a sudden one of the brown sharks just snapped it in two. It's something that happens in nature—survival of the fittest. If a fish is sick, it's fair game. The biggest problem was that I couldn't do a necropsy to find out what was wrong."

Doctoring the Fish

Once a diagnosis has been made, there are several ways to treat a sick fish: give it medicine by mouth; give it a needle; or put the medicine in the water. Medicine in the water can treat the outside of the fish, the way we would spray antiseptic on a wound, or it can be taken into the bloodstream through the gills.

Even once they're treated, fish are not necessarily rid of parasites. If only a few survive on even one host, they can multiply and reinfect the whole tank. The only way to wipe them out completely is to remove all the hosts and treat both them and the tank, just

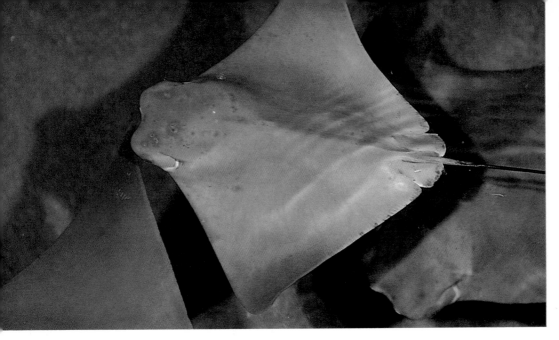

Aquarists had to scoop more than 20 cownose rays out of the Open Ocean tank for medical treatment.

as you might have a dog dipped to kill its fleas and treat your house at the same time.

But Frank has found that this is nearly impossible to do.

"Right now all the cownose rays are infected with a parasitic worm. You can see small worms embedded in their eyelids," he points out as a ray glides by. "The worms are not deadly, but the rays end up scratching themselves, and then the wounds get .infected."

The ray bumps awkwardly along the ocean floor, scraping itself on the gravelly bottom.

"This worm only affects rays—it has no effect on the other fish. But it's hard to get rid of because it has different life stages. In one stage, it's on the ray. Then it drops its eggs to the gravel. We can treat the ones on the rays, but then the ones in the gravel come up in the water column. The only way to really get rid of them is to remove the rays from the tank for about thirty days so when the worms hatch and come up, they find nothing to attach to, and they die."

But getting all the rays out of the tank is no simple task.

"We tried it. We strung barrier nets across the whole tank and corralled most of the rays into the holding tank. Then we got some of the others out by standing on the dive platform and scooping them up with dip nets when they swam by. But if we missed them the first time, they got wise, and there were a few we just couldn't get out." Those few were enough to keep the parasites breeding, and now the whole process must be repeated.

"The key to keeping a collection healthy is not in treatment; it's in prevention. That means providing excellent water quality and nutrition and designing exhibits that support natural behaviors," says Frank.

ALL IN A DAY'S WORK

6

The building is filled with a frenzy of activity in the weeks and days before the opening, as workers rush to put the finishing touches on each exhibit. From now on, the aquarists must do everything from feeding the animals to caring for the live plants in the exhibits and keeping the windows sparkling clean—from the inside.

Standing knee-deep in the waters of the Pine Barrens exhibit, aquarist Randy Mickley fills up the entire window. He steps gently, careful not to tread on a frog or a turtle as he tends to his newest addition—three pitcher plants scavenged from a flower show.

"A local greenhouse had a display of native plants, and they let us have these when the show was over. I think they make this exhibit a lot more interesting. Pitcher plants are one of three kinds of carnivorous, or meat-eating, plants—the others are Venus's-flytraps and sundews," he explains. Living in the nitrogen-poor soil of the Pines, the pitcher plants eat insects to get the nitrogen they need.

Gently lifting a leaf of goldenseal from under the water, he points to bite marks all over it.

"I think it's the turtle. That ingrate! I feed him every day, and this is the thanks I get," he says.

Seeing a smudge on the inside of the window, he wipes it clean with a soft cloth.

Banded sunfish dart anxiously about his legs, but the southern leopard frogs just sit like bumps on their artificial logs, apparently oblivious to the intrusion.

"I'm going to have to put these frogs on a diet because they're getting so fat—they just sit here and eat," he says as he climbs out of the tank.

The octopus is a clever creature.

Eight-armed Houdini

Upstairs, education staffer Paul Taylor has discovered that even a simple job like changing a light bulb can be exciting when there's an octopus involved. Reaching in to grab the bulb, he was grabbed by a long, strong tentacle.

"I told him the octopus would probably come up to him," says aquarist Mike Sokol. "I've been feeding that fellow by hand—squid, scallops, crabs. First I dangle the food in the water and let him get a tentacle on it; then I pull. It keeps life interesting for him. He's very strong. He'll grab you with one tentacle, then as soon as you pull that one off yourself, another one comes up. It's kind of like fighting with a bowl of spaghetti that has a mind"—a mind with an appetite for escape.

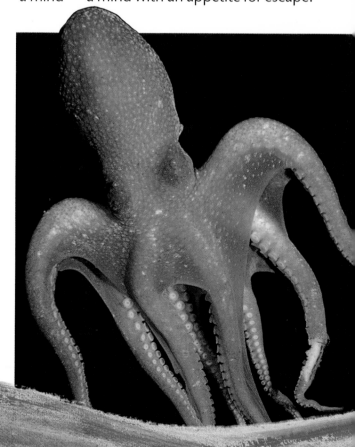

The octopus has no bones or cartilage; the only hard part of its body is its beak. It can puff up its flexible body with water like a big balloon, or squeeze the water out and flatten itself. Like a scarf pulled from a magician's sleeve, this eight-armed Houdini can squeeze through any opening its beak can fit through—on average, the size of a man's thumb. Even a hundred-pounder with an eight-foot arm span can stretch thin like a rubber band, flatten itself, and squeeze its flexible body through the smallest crack.

If another tank is nearby, this night prowler may visit and nibble on its neighbors—or it could wind up falling on the floor and dying.

"At one aquarium where I worked, all the tanks were up against each other. Once the octopus got out, it would go into another tank and eat what it wanted, then go into another tank, and so on—until we discovered that it hated Astroturf," says Brian DuVall.

For unknown reasons, the octopus will not cross Astroturf, so its tank is rimmed with the stuff to keep it from roaming.

Rainbow Seas

Around the corner from the octopus tank, Mike tends to the Rainbow Seas exhibit, a seven-hundred-gallon tank that holds live corals and tropical fish.

Although it looks like a rocky hillside blanketed by a crazy-quilt garden of beautiful, exotic plants, a coral reef is really made up of hundreds of tiny animals.

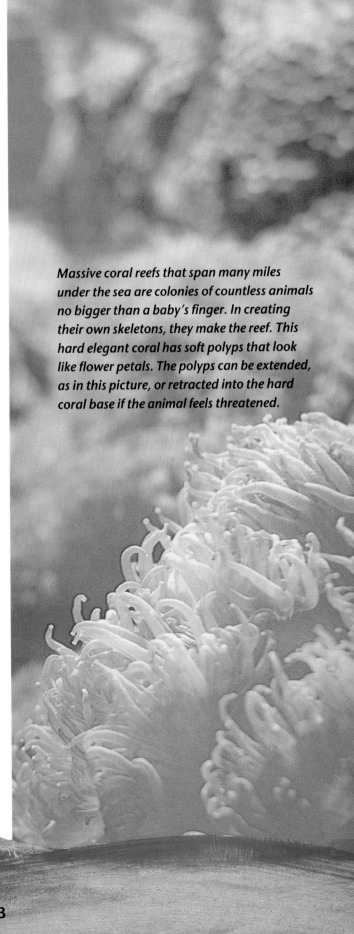

Massive coral reefs that span many miles under the sea are colonies of countless animals no bigger than a baby's finger. In creating their own skeletons, they make the reef. This hard elegant coral has soft polyps that look like flower petals. The polyps can be extended, as in this picture, or retracted into the hard coral base if the animal feels threatened.

Those rocks are the corals' own skeletons, created by limestonelike secretions. The corals' soft polyps extend from the skeletons, swaying in the water current like flower petals. The current carries food to the animals, which are anchored in place, and it washes away their wastes. Because corals can't swim away, their only self-defense is to close up suddenly if a fish begins to nibble on them, or if Mike dips his hand into the tank to add a coral or make a change.

"When the polyps retract, the flowerpot coral looks like a head of broccoli," he says.

Putting new corals into the tank is a lot like arranging flowers, trying to find just the right spot to show off each one's beauty. But he

On a crowded coral reef, color talks. Wearing their family colors, fish easily spot their own kind. Mating fish display their brightest colors. Some colors spell poison to those in the know.

go on one after another, to imitate the movement of the sun. And the temperature is carefully regulated so it doesn't vary more than a few degrees.

Mike also has to be careful about which fish he puts in this tank. In the wild, a coral reef is alive with crazily striped and spotted tropical fish, but some of them eat the coral. That's all right on a big reef, but in a small tank, it's a problem. "Clownfish and firefish are okay, but parrotfish, butterflyfish, and angelfish will eat the coral," he says.

One thing Mike doesn't have to worry much about is feeding the corals. Many have their own food source living inside them.

"All the hard corals have tiny plants, called zooxanthellae algae, living inside them," Mike says.

Through photosynthesis, the algae use sunlight to recycle the carbon dioxide that the coral polyps give off as waste, turning it back into food for the coral. The algae also give the corals their spectacular colors. That's why if a coral is plucked from the ocean, its colors soon fade. The algae inside die out of water. Without the algae, the coral animal dies too.

also has to keep the animals healthy. "Some need more light, some less, some like a little more water movement, so I place them higher or lower, depending on what they need and where they fit," Mike says.

Corals are delicate animals that grow slowly and are a challenge to keep alive in captivity. The tank is lit by three bulbs timed to

When this sailfin tang turns sideways, its bright stripes are hard to miss, but head-on it's so thin it almost disappears.

"Working with a small coral tank really gives you an appreciation for how fragile reefs are," Mike says. Because they take so long to grow and are so easily damaged, even a vast underwater expanse like the Great Barrier Reef, which stretches for more than twelve hundred miles off Australia's shores, is vulnerable to destruction by careless divers and boaters.

While Mike relies on the algae inside the corals to feed them, algae in the tank is another thing. In addition to clouding the view, an excess of algae in the surrounding water can smother the coral.

A sailfin tang and a team of snails act as the tank's live-in housekeepers. Mike also adds a few drops of marine tank clarifier, a solution sold in pet shops that kills algae. It does not harm the algae inside the coral, because they're sheltered by their hosts.

Housekeeping in the Deep

Once the aquarium is open to the public, most of the cleaning and maintenance of displays will be done early in the morning, before the aquarium opens. One exception is the Open Ocean tank.

"We'll be cleaning the inside of the window and the rocks and shipwreck after dive shows because people like to watch us," says Skip Uricchio, who with Marc Kind and Fran Ansbro is in charge of caring for and feeding all the fish in the ocean tank. Before today's first dive, Skip stands on the narrow catwalk that rims the top of the ocean tank to check out a seven-foot brown shark that has just been moved from the warehouse into the holding tank.

"She looks like a big 747," he says as the shark cruises below him, fins extended from her sides like airplane wings.

"See how sleek she is? That's how they're supposed to look," he says.

Each shark is fed about three pounds of fish every other day. Marc and Skip lure them to the holding area and offer them fish on the end of a twenty-foot-long pole—a routine

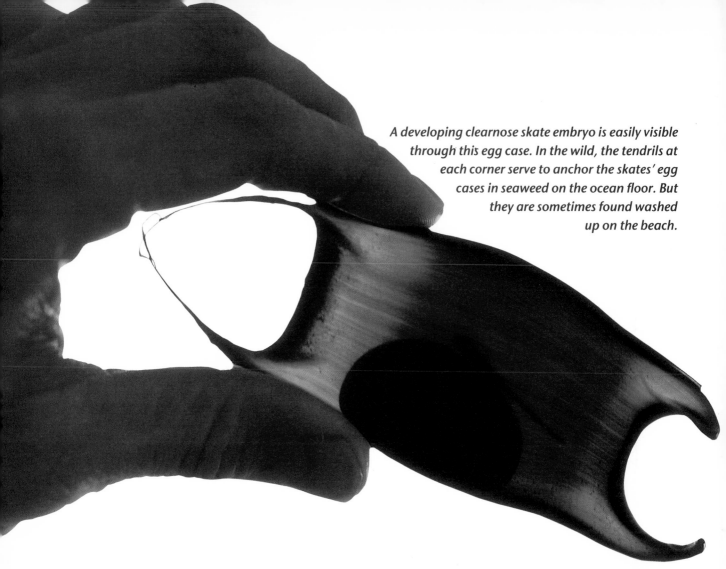

A developing clearnose skate embryo is easily visible through this egg case. In the wild, the tendrils at each corner serve to anchor the skates' egg cases in seaweed on the ocean floor. But they are sometimes found washed up on the beach.

they've gotten used to at the warehouse. Besides making it possible to examine the sharks, this helps to ensure that each shark is eating as it should. So far, it seems to be working.

"The sharks have had a couple of midnight snacks—not many," Skip says. If there were seals in this exhibit, he says, fish would disappear daily. "Seals hunt for sport. They would harass the fish and play with them. The sharks eat just to eat. They don't do it for fun."

"Some aquariums use divers to feed the fish. We don't, because we don't want the sharks to associate the divers with food," Fran says, joining Skip on the catwalk.

The sharks can be somewhat aggressive towards the divers. "On my last dive, the big female sand tiger came from behind me, swam over my shoulder, turned to look at me, and extended her jaws," Skip says. "We couldn't get the sharks out of the Abyss—they were buzzing us like bomber pilots."

Divers here observe one of the cardinal rules of scuba training: Never go in without a buddy.

Even when they're not aggressive, some of the fish are just plain curious. "The rays swim right up to your mask, then veer away. And the puffers nip at your fins," Skip says.

Now he and Fran climb down onto the dive platform and pull on their weight belts, tanks, masks, and fins. Then they splash into the tank feet-first. They submerge quickly.

While Skip cleans algae off the rocks with a paintbrush, Fran keeps an eye out for the sharks. One big sand tiger swims straight towards Fran, skimming little more than a foot over her head as she sinks down in the water.

When Skip comes up, he carries a couple of skate egg cases—small, tough brown rectangles with a slim tendril coming from each corner. The skates have been mating in the big tank. Holding a case up to the light, Skip points out the round egg sac that provides food, and the small, wriggling embryo beside it.

"Inside the case, they're folded up like burritos," Skip says. "When they come out, they unfold, and they look exactly like adult skates, only miniature."

The egg cases Skip retrieves will be incubated and hatched for display in the Water Babies exhibit upstairs. Because they have such tough cases, the skate babies have a better chance at survival than most of the other newborn fish would here in the ocean tank.

"The tautogs have also been spawning in the Abyss," Skip says, pointing out two fish swimming fast and close together. "It looks like they're chasing each other, but they're actually doing more. The males swim around the female. Then they bolt to mid-water, and the female ejects her eggs. The males swim into the cloud and eject sperm to fertilize the eggs," Skip says. "The chances of any of the young surviving are very slim. All the other fish dash in right away and eat the eggs."

Chop Fish and Dream

Downstairs, Denise Cornwell is in the food preparation room chopping lake smelt into small pieces. All the fish except the sharks are fed once a day.

"Fortunately this is not the only aspect of the job," Denise says, wielding a big butcher knife. She is a college student, working a few hours a week at the aquarium to get some on-the-job experience and course credits.

"I like the fact that it's not a usual job—you learn something new every day. It's almost like playing," she says. A certified scuba diver, she hopes to join the aquarium's volunteer diving program.

"It's like studying outer space, the unknown," Denise says. "There are a lot of similarities—the weightlessness underwater, the fact that you're not even breathing on your own. You see things you've never seen before. It's a totally different world."

7 THE BENEFITS OF BLUBBER

Outside, it's a nippy February morning, but that doesn't stop Luke and Squeegee from taking a swim in the 52° Fahrenheit waters of their private 170,000-gallon swimming pool. Weighing in at close to two hundred pounds each, they're a bit on the plump side, but no one is mentioning diets to these two fellows.

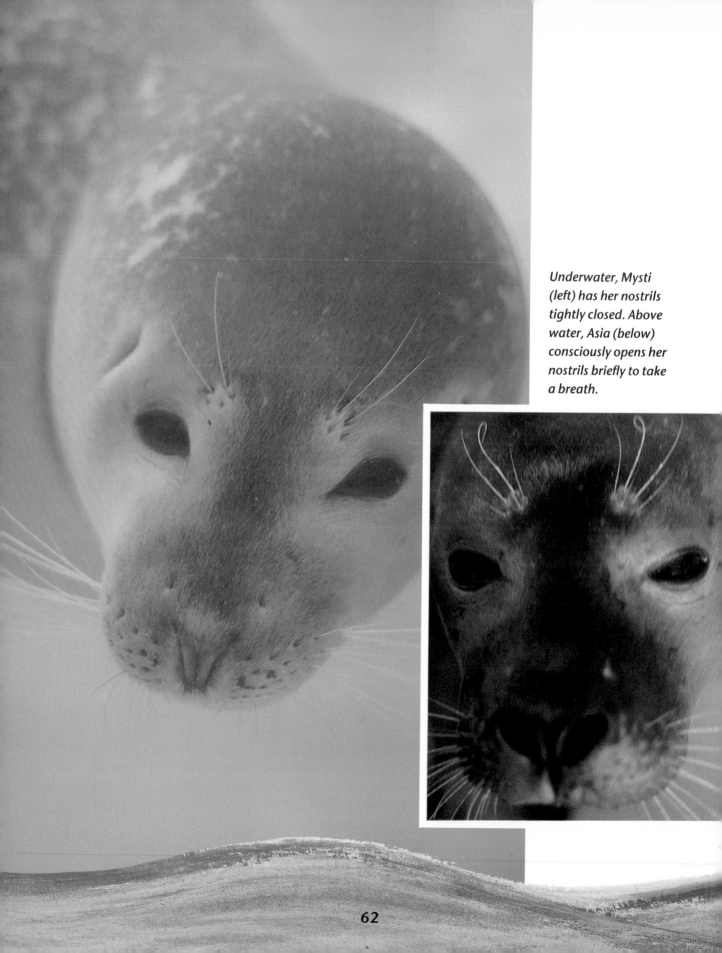

Underwater, Mysti (left) has her nostrils tightly closed. Above water, Asia (below) consciously opens her nostrils briefly to take a breath.

Blubber is a blessing to seals. These animals live most of their lives in the water, although they are air-breathing mammals like people. Their blubber insulates their bodies like a warm coat, protecting them from the cold. It also helps them float, so they can nap near the surface of the water, breathing easily as they bob up and down.

They are protected from getting a nose full of water while napping because the natural position of a seal's nostrils is closed. The seal must open its nostrils when it wants to breathe. If it relaxes its muscles, its nostrils will snap shut.

Luke and Squeegee are harbor seals, a kind found from Greenland all the way down the east coasts of Canada and the United States, and from the Yukon and northern Alaska south to the California coast. They can dive as deep as three hundred feet and hold their breath for almost half an hour.

Their pool at the aquarium is only eight feet at its deepest point, but that's deep enough for Luke and Squeegee to do some speed swimming, "porpoising," and frolicking around the pool.

This morning, Squeegee zooms back and forth along a big underwater window, following the motions of a worker washing the window as if to engage him in play.

The man chuckles. "He just loves to play this game. And there's the upside-down swimmer," he points out as Luke swims into sight from the other part of the pool.

The belly-up swimming position Luke prefers is actually a good hunting position for a seal. When he is upside down, he can look down and see fish lit up by the sunlight coming in from overhead.

Putting on Pounds

Inside the small seal-holding building behind the seal pool, trainer Jean Joseph is making breakfast according to a menu posted above her head:

Luke 10:30 A.M. feeding
2 1/2 lbs. herring
1 1/2 lbs. mackerel
1/4 lb. capelin

Luke chows down on more than twelve pounds of fish a day at this time of year, hand-fed by trainers careful to make sure he eats enough.

"The seals' diets are based on each animal's body weight, the calorie content of the fish, and the time of year," Jean says. "In fall and winter they get more, to try to build them up." In the summer, Luke's diet will be cut down to between four and six pounds a day.

Jean stands over a deep stainless-steel sink, sorting and washing whole herring. "I'm making sure each fish is firm, with no rips or tears, or anything that breaks into the body cavity. We can't feed them that. Fish have a great deal of bacteria on their skin. If a cut breaks into the body cavity, it gives the bacteria a chance to grow."

She tosses one with a deep gash in its belly into a big plastic trash can. Good ones are placed in a clear plastic box, then weighed into portions for each seal.

"In the wild they would eat a variety of fish. They're probably not as picky as we are in choosing their food. What they get here is considered restaurant quality."

She weighs out Luke's portion, then puts the fish into a stainless-steel bucket. "Usually we hide their vitamins in the first fish of the day—one multivitamin, two B, and two E vitamins," Jean says.

To keep them regular, the seals eat squid twice a week. Squid is the prune of the sea—it provides roughage in the seals' diet.

Senior seal trainer Rhona St. Clair knocks, and Jean lets her in. The doors are locked from the inside for security. Just inside the door is a shallow tray with Astroturf and about an inch of disinfectant in it for cleaning shoes. Rhona steps into this, then steps out and dries her shoes on a towel.

"This is required by law," Jean says. "Marine mammals are the only federally regulated animals. There are regulations on everything, from transporting the animals to water quality, exhibit size, depth of the pool, size of haul-out areas, sterilization of food preparation areas, and overall cleanliness."

Waiting in the Wings

In addition to Luke and Squeegee outside, three more seals are waiting in the wings—going through a period of adjustment in the

holding building which has two five-foot-deep pools in it.

The three seals in the holding building will get salt tablets in addition to their vitamins, because their pools have fresh water in them. The outdoor pool is on a separate, saltwater system.

Seals can live in either salt water or fresh water. In the spring, when salmon are running upriver, harbor seals may follow them for many hundreds of miles before returning to the sea.

Rhona slides open the gate that separates the holding pool from the walkway. To her right are two gray seal sisters: eight-year-old Kara and one-year-old Kjya. To her left is the baby of the bunch—a nine-month-old harbor seal called Mysti.

Kara hauls out right away; using her strong rear flippers, she pushes herself up out of the water, sliding easily onto the concrete area beside her pool. When she sees Rhona going to the other end, she jumps back into the pool and hauls out on the other side.

While Rhona carefully scrubs down the enclosure, Kara and Kjya go around and around, gleefully exploring the area usually closed off to them. They peer through the gate at Mysti.

New seals brought in from the wild are kept separated for 30 days to make sure they are not carrying any diseases.

After they play for about ten minutes, the gates are closed and Mysti's are opened. But she is not as bold and has to be coaxed to haul out even for food. She zooms around her pool, eyeing Rhona while her area is scrubbed down.

Now it's breakfast time.

Rhona opens the gate and goes in to Mysti. "You're okay," she says reassuringly. She puts a dog whistle in her mouth, hands Mysti a small chunk of fish, and blows a short tweet. The seals learn early to respond to the whistle, which forms the basis for a lot of their training.

"Every time we feed them a piece of fish, we bridge it with a whistle so they get used to hearing the whistle with food and associate the sound with a positive experience," Rhona says. Mysti takes the fish, dives, and comes up with it still in her mouth, then tosses it up and eats it.

"Good girl," Rhona says, putting another fish in Mysti's mouth and giving a short, high tweet on the whistle. This time, when Mysti comes up, she still has the fish in her mouth.

"Mysti is very aware that these fish can't get away," Jean says. "She'll drop it on the bottom, pick it up under her flipper, and swim to the top to fool us into thinking she's eaten it."

The seals have very playful personalities.

"One day Kara and I had a pulling contest with the gate—I would close it and she would

65

nose it open again before I could latch it," Jean says. "She's a real character."

Kara and Kjya play, nipping at each other. Kjya rolls into the pool. She is not eating her fish heads, so Jean cuts them off and tosses them.

"At this point we're being very accommodating with their eating habits, although there's no reason for them not to eat the heads—they would eat the whole fish in the wild," Rhona says.

The herring they are getting are about a foot long, about a third of a pound each—"Just the size for pickled herring," Jean says.

Like dogs, the seals get heartworm preventive medicine once a month.

While Rhona feeds Kara and Kjya, Jean carefully scrubs down the sink in the food preparation area.

"Everything that gets touched gets scrubbed, then hosed down," Jean says. "We use a surgical scrub. Once a week we bleach everything. Most people are very surprised at the amount of cleaning we do."

"Yeah, I wanted to be a marine mammal trainer," Rhona says wryly. "Everybody thinks this job is so glamorous. It is fun, but it's also a lot of grunt work."

Seals at School

It's 10:30 A.M. Time for the first of four daily feedings outside.

Rhona and Jean put on cotton gloves covered with latex gloves to protect their hands from the cold. Each grabs a stainless-steel bucket, and they head outside to feed Luke and Squeegee.

They come out onto the rocks at the upper part of the pool. Squeegee goes to Rhona right away. Rhona feeds him a piece of fish, whistles.

The goal here at the aquarium is to show visitors the skills the animals use in the wild. "When they play or frolic, they're very agile swimmers," Rhona says. "They 'porpoise' when they're excited or in pursuit of fish, swimming fast and rising above the water."

The seals are trained to respond to rewards and to the sound of a whistle, like the one Rhona St. Clair is using above.

The outdoor pool is designed to give visitors an idea of the kind of rocky, sandy shoreline, with beach grasses and dunes surrounding it, where seals would live in the wild. There are both above-water and underwater views of the seals in action.

Some of the training here is aimed at getting the animals to haul out and willingly undergo a checkup: having their bellies, mouths, and flippers checked, and having blood taken when necessary. This ensures that the trainers and the vet will be able to examine them regularly. Wild animals that are hurt or injured will instinctively hide their injury, so it's important that the trainers keep a close watch on the seals to spot any problems that need attention.

Rhona holds out her fist. Squeegee puts his nose up to it. Rhona gestures, spreading her thumb and forefinger apart. Squeegee opens his mouth, giving her a chance to look at his gums and teeth.

"To train him to do this, I started by touching his jaw, one finger on top, thumb on the bottom jaw, and prying it open a little," Rhona says. "When he relaxed his jaw and his mouth dropped open a little, I would blow the whistle, then give him a piece of fish.

"Having them touch the fist is called targeting," Rhona explains. "It's having the animal focus on the trainer. We want to have them always following the target, so if it moves left, they move left. It's the basis for a lot of behaviors.

"You put your fist up. When the animal touches its nose to the fist, you whistle and give a reward. Then you expand from there. You ask them not only to target but to hold—stay where they are. In training, we don't

The Seal Shores exhibit re-creates the look of a sandy coastline. It is divided into two sections with a gate between that can be closed for maintenance or to separate some animals from the others. Visitors can see the seals frolicking from above water or through underwater viewing windows.

punish our animals if they don't do what we want. We do a time-out—take our attention away.

"When I was training Squeegee to roll over, I did aversion training. Seals don't like to be touched. So I'd put my hand on his belly and he'd roll away; then I'd whistle and give him a reward."

Being bitten is not a big concern, she says—despite the mouth full of strong, sharp teeth Squeegee just displayed.

"They can bite, but if you're working with them properly and not antagonizing them, there's no reason they should bite."

After feeding Luke and Squeegee, Rhona and Jean coax Kara and Kjya partway out of the holding building to have a look around. Soon, the two will move outside permanently. At first they will go into the deeper section of the pool, with a see-through gate between them and the two male seals so they can get acquainted.

"As soon as we see that there are no signs of aggression through the gate and that everybody is eating properly, we will put them together," Rhona says.

Safety First

All the seals in this group were born in captivity. Eventually, the aquarium may work with the Marine Mammal Stranding Network, taking in stranded animals that cannot be released into the wild.

"Seals that are young when they are stranded, because they were separated from their mothers or because their mothers were killed, haven't learned to survive in the wild," says Brian DuVall. "Those that need a lot of medical attention have often had too much contact with humans, or their injuries are too disabling, for them to be released."

Often seals are stranded because they have been injured by killer whales or sharks. Sometimes they have been hit by boats, have gunshot wounds, or are tangled in fishing line or plastic six-pack rings. Seals may also eat balloons or plastic bags, which can suffocate them or damage their digestive systems.

Even the seals at the aquarium are at risk, from people throwing objects into their pool. An education staffer or volunteer will always be posted near the seal pool to make sure nothing is thrown in.

If anything does fall into the pool, it will be removed immediately. Seals are very curious creatures, and a coin or toy tossed into the pool may prove irresistible—and deadly.

8
A NEW ANGLE ON SEA LIFE

Opening day is here at last! Huge helium balloons in the shapes of starfish and seals twirl on the waterfront outside the aquarium. Children costumed as sea creatures sing nautical tunes, and a band plays "Victory at Sea." The governor wields a huge pair of scissors to slice a wave-shaped ribbon, and the crowds pour in for their first glimpse of the new aquarium.

The day's activities will close with a celebratory burst of fireworks tonight. But all this is just a passing thrill. The seven thousand people here on opening day have really come to witness the mysteries of the deep.

To Touch a Shark

"How many people want to touch a shark?" volunteer guide Judie Weinstein asks a crowd pressed around the waist-high shark-touch tank. A wave of excitement ripples through the crowd as some cry "Me!" while others shrink back in horror.

"Roll up your sleeves and get ready. Wait until the shark's head has passed you, then slide your hand along its back. If you put your hand in the water or hang over the water, it will see you and veer away."

Two sharks, smooth dogfish about three feet long, swim around and around the tank, bobbing up at the sides, where visitors wait for a chance to stroke them. A pair of cownose rays and several clearnose skates lie like dinner plates on the bottom, fluttering only rarely to the top.

"It feels like sandpaper!" says visitor Erin Fischer after gliding her hand along a shark's back.

"The shark's skin is made of tiny, toothlike scales that are called denticles," Judie explains. "That's why it feels so rough."

It's no coincidence that the shark-touch tank is one of the first exhibits visitors come

Visitors thrill at the chance to stroke a small shark or ray. A hand splashing in the water might attract some sharks, but it makes smooth dogfish shy away.

to at the aquarium. Sharks are a must-see at any aquarium—one of its biggest attractions. They are also the most misunderstood, which is why this aquarium is giving visitors a chance to get to know them up close—and hands-on.

getting—odors, tastes, vibrations. It puts all that together to find things around it that are good to eat."

The smooth dogfish in the touch tank are bottom feeders whose idea of a good meal is shrimp or crab. They have small, blunt teeth that work well for crushing shells—not for biting off hands.

"Even if people splash their hands around, these sharks don't respond," Brian says. Visitors at the touch tank are closely supervised—to make sure they don't harm the sharks.

Even to the big sand tigers and brown sharks in the Open Ocean tank, people don't look like lunch.

"Certain things attract sharks: blood in the water, the kind of vibrations fish make when they are injured, any kind of abnormal swimming style," Brian says.

All these things tell a shark it has found an easy target—which may be why swimmers and bathers in shallow water sometimes attract the unwelcome attention of sharks. A person swimming on the surface, or splashing and jumping up and down, probably makes a lot of vibrations similar to an injured fish. That's why it's important to stay out of the water if a shark is spotted nearby.

Sharks are the most efficient predators in the sea. They can sniff out a drop of blood in a hundred thousand gallons of water. They also have a keen sense of hearing, both

"We want to debunk some of the myths about sharks," says Director of Husbandry Brian DuVall. "People think of a shark as being mean and aggressive, but it's not. A shark, most of the time, is probably looking for food. It's processing the information it's through an inner ear that is a lot like our own and through the lateral line, an organ unique to fish.

The lateral line is a series of canals buried just under the skin along the length of the body. It is filled with a jellylike substance that helps the fish sense even slight vibrations in the water. Schooling fish rely on vibrations sensed through the lateral line to keep from bumping into one another. In dark waters, fish use it to feel their way around. Sharks use it to zero in on their prey.

A shark can find even well-hidden, motionless prey. It can find a flounder half-buried in the sand by detecting the tiny electric impulses its breathing creates. Special electromagnetic sensors, the ampullae of Lorenzini, in the shark's face, pick up those impulses and help the shark home in for the kill.

Seeing with Sound

Chris and Jason Fischer bound up the stairs to the aquarium's second floor. At the top, an abstract sculpture of a dolphin's head gives them a chance to try out echolocation, or dolphin sonar.

Chris puts his head inside the sculpture and immediately hears a clicking sound in one ear. A few seconds later, the echo of that sound returns in the other ear after bouncing off a nearby wall. When Jason stands right in front of him, the echo comes back much faster.

Dolphins make rapid clicking sounds, sending them out at rates of from twenty to a thousand per second and listening for the echoes to form a sound image of their surroundings. They can detect a school of fish almost a mile away in only two seconds, and can tell what kind of fish they are.

Dolphins also use sonar to find their way in deep or murky waters. Low-frequency clicks provide a broad view; more-rapid clicks fill in the details.

Next to the dolphin's head is a tank with no fish in it—only an underwater speaker. Chris and Jason press their hands against the side of a tank. They can't hear the music, but through the palms of their hands they can feel the beat.

CAN YOU NAME THAT TUNE? reads the display sign.

"Give up?" Chris asks. Jason nods and pushes a button, to hear James Brown singing "I Feel Good."

A fish can hear, or sense the vibrations sound makes in water, two ways—through the lateral line, and through its ears.

Some fish can "talk," making loud noises scientists believe may be mating calls or distress signals. The sea is alive with the grunts and whistles of toadfish and the sounds of catfish "singing."

Red drums and black drums get their common name from the loud sounds they make. People above water have reported being able to hear black drums thumping from sixty feet underwater.

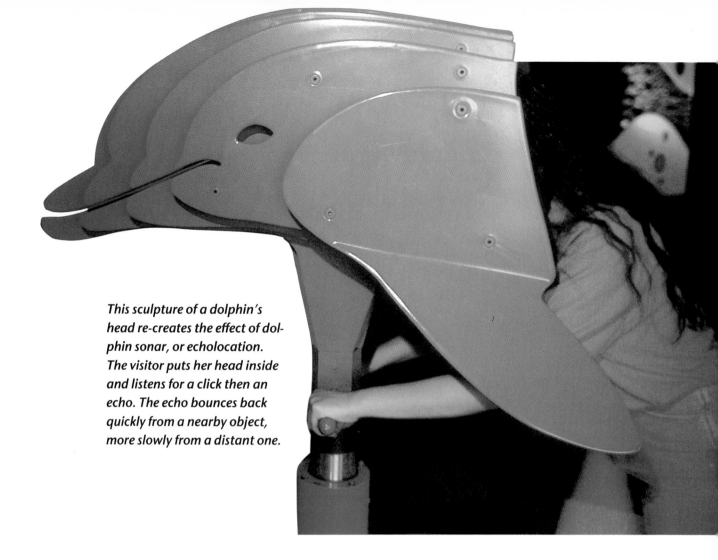

This sculpture of a dolphin's head re-creates the effect of dolphin sonar, or echolocation. The visitor puts her head inside and listens for a click then an echo. The echo bounces back quickly from a nearby object, more slowly from a distant one.

The Body Electric

"Watch me test my muscle power," Michael Quinn tells his father. He puts his arm in a cradle designed to pick up electrical impulses, makes a fist, and then relaxes it. A green wave bounces and curves on an oscilloscope screen overhead, showing how much power he's generating.

Every living thing produces electrical energy. Some animals, like the electric eel or northern stargazer, can use the energy to deliver a stunning blow to their next meal. Others, like sharks and rays, will home in on the energy created by an unwitting flounder just breathing on the bottom. And some fish are like underwater ham-radio operators, able to both send and receive signals.

Led by Their Noses

Caroline Rieders spins a big metal drum, waits for it to stop, then leans toward it to take a multiple-choice sniff test.

All living creatues produce electrical energy, but a few, like this electric eel, can produce an electric shock to stun their prey. Electric eels can produce up to 650 volts to stun or kill small fish or frogs, which they then swallow whole. They also use their electric abilities to find their way around and to protect themselves from predators. The average lightbulb uses 120 volts of electricity, so an electric eel could power five bulbs, enough to light up a small house.

"What do you smell?" asks Jennifer Warren.

Caroline reads her choices from the wheel:
In the Woods
At the Zoo
Let's Have Lunch

She presses the button next to *In the Woods* and a picture of pine trees lights up below.

"Good sense of smell!" Jennifer says.

Some fish can sniff out the scent of fear or food, or follow a trail like a bloodhound would. News, in the form of different odors, travels fast underwater. Scents produced by sexually active fish, blood, wastes, and normal body odors make the water a potpourri of current events. More things can be smelled underwater than in the air because more substances dissolve in water.

In a kitchen just before dinner the air is filled with the smell of onions cooking, rolls baking, flowers on the table, and the wet fur of a dog that has just come in out of the rain.

But if the kitchen were underwater, so much more could be smelled. All the spice jars in the cabinet would give off strong scents; the paint on the walls would start seeping into the water; the wet wood would give off an odor; the dishwashing liquid would dissolve; and blood would seep out of the raw chicken sitting on the counter.

Some fish have a "chemical language," releasing a different pheromone, or scent, for each message. When catfish and minnows are injured, they give off special scents that trigger fright responses in their companions, who quickly scatter.

Atlantic lobsters use one scent to tell if another lobster is male or female, another to signal that they are ready for a fight, and yet another to say they are ready to mate. Lobsters have poor eyesight, so they rely on smell to figure out what's going on.

Who's Looking at You?

"Look! I'm on TV!" says Aharon Wasserman.

Three television screens, mounted over three different tanks, show him how he looks to the animals in the tank.

An emperor angelfish swims slowly around the first tank; overhead, the screen shows a crisp color image—Aharon recognizes himself easily.

"What happened to you here? You look like a split personality," his father jokes, pointing to the screen over the lobster's tank, where the picture looks like a jigsaw puzzle gone wrong.

Lobsters have compound eyes, just as flies do. A fine-lined grid divides the lobster's eyes into many light-sensitive facets. Each facet sends a message to the brain, which adds up all the messages to create a mosaic image.

"I'm just a blur," says Gina Roswell, pointing to the screen over the squirrelfish.

"This fish lives deep in the ocean and feeds at night, so it's not used to a lot of light," her mother says. "It can see that you're moving, but not much more—like when you get up in the middle of the night, and there are no lights on."

In places where light is scarce, vision gives way to the other senses; smell, taste and touch take over. Deep-sea fish are often drably colored, and some are virtually blind. But color is a vital part of life for the fish that live on sun-drenched coral reefs. Here, color talks—and it helps get the message across quickly. Wearing their "family colors," fish easily spot their own kind, and mating fish display their brightest colors.

Color can also camouflage a fish, allowing it to hide from predators or surprise its prey.

Tiffany Hamm lifts a foot-long flounder magnet off a colorful wall mural. Adrenee Robinson takes a slim red trumpetfish magnet. "It's a giant game of hide-and-seek," Tiffany says. "You find a place for the fish to hide."

She finds a home for the flounder on the ocean floor, where its spots match the sandy bottom.

Adrenee discovers that the trumpetfish vanishes when it is hung head-down among some soft red coral.

Looking less fishy can be a great advantage in a fish-eat-fish world. Hunter and hunted alike use camouflage as a survival tactic. And some, like the octopus, can change colors completely. Sometimes it changes to match its surroundings; other times the changes reflect its mood.

Enjoying a crab dinner in its tank at the aquarium, the giant Pacific octopus may turn a bright red. When it first arrived on the airplane, it was white as a ghost from the stress of the flight. But now, on opening day, it's so comfortable that visitors must look closely to find it curled up in a corner of the tank, as brown as the rocks around it.

And visitors do take the time to look for the shy deep sea creature. But now the crowds are thinning, as opening day draws to a close. In the days and years to come, thousands more will come to marvel and delight at this splendid display of aquatic life—brought inside for all to share at the aquarium.

A catfish has so many taste buds on its body and its barbels, or whiskers, that it is like a swimming tongue, taste-testing everything that floats by.